278498

92
,AS
$22.00

S0-BZG-465

A FIREFLY BIOLOGIST AT WORK

Sneed B. Collard III

A Wildlife Conservation Society Book

Franklin Watts
A Division of Scholastic Inc.
New York • Toronto • London • Auckland • Sydney
Mexico City • New Delhi • Hong Kong
Danbury, Connecticut

The Wildlife Conservation Society (WCS) is dedicated to protecting and promoting the world's wildlife and wilderness areas. Founded in 1895 as the New York Zoological Society, the organization operates the Bronx Zoo, New York Aquarium, Central Park Wildlife Center, Queens Wildlife Center, and Prospect Park Wildlife Center. WCS also operates St. Catherines Wildlife Center, which is located off the coast of Georgia. The scientists at this center raise and study a variety of threatened and endangered animals.

WCS currently sponsors more than 350 field projects in 52 countries. The goal of these projects is to save wild landscapes and the animals that depend on them. In addition, WCS's pioneering environmental education programs reach more than 3 million students in the New York metropolitan area and are used in all 50 states and 14 foreign nations.

For John and Elisabeth Buck,
pioneers of science and spirit

Library of Congress Cataloging-in-Publication Data

Collard, Sneed B.
    A firefly biologist at work / Sneed B. Collard III.
        p. cm.– (A Wildlife Conservation Society Book)
    Includes bibliographical references and index.
    ISBN 0-531-11798-7 (lib. bdg.)   0-531-16568-X (pbk.)
    1. Case, James F., 1926—Juvenile literature. 2. Biologists—United States—
Biography—Juvenile literature. 3. Fireflies—Juvenile literature. [1. Case, James F.,
1926- 2. Biologists. 3. Fireflies.] I. Title.

QH31.C345 C66   2001
595.76'44–dc21
[B]
                                                                00-29622

GROLIER
PUBLISHING

©2001 Sneed B. Collard III
All rights reserved. Published simultaneously in Canada.
Printed in the United States of America.
1 2 3 4 5 6 7 8 9 10 R 10 09 08 07 06 05 04 03 02 01

CONTENTS

MEET THE AUTHOR

Author Sneed B. Collard enjoys any adventure that can teach him something about the natural world. This photograph was taken during a whale watch off the coast of California.

Sneed B. Collard III is the author of more than two dozen books for young people. Before beginning his writing career, Sneed graduated with honors in marine biology from the University of California at Berkeley. Today, he lives in Missoula, Montana, but often travels to research his books and to speak to children and educators about writing, science, and environmental protection. To learn more about Sneed's books, school visits, and other activities, check out his Web site at *http://www.author-illustr-source.com/ sneedbcollard.htm.*

"In 1975, when I was 15 years old and traveling overseas for the first time, a man took me to a river in southern Malaysia," recalls Sneed. "It was a trip I will never forget. We arrived at a tiny village and climbed into a boat that was so tipsy it almost capsized every

time I glanced over the side. As dusk set in, fruit bats as big as crows flapped overhead and tropical birds called from the surrounding forest.

"Soon, I noticed bright yellow-green flashes of fireflies from the branches of the mangrove trees along the river. As the sky darkened, more and

Sneed Collard has fond memories of his trip to Malaysia. He was fascinated by the fireflies he saw there.

more fireflies flashed. Then, something amazing happened. All the fireflies—tens of thousands of them—started flashing at once. FLASH! FLASH! FLASH! They turned the riverbanks into giant streaks of lightning that permanently burned themselves into my memory.

"The man who took me to that river more than 25 years ago is my stepfather, Professor James F. Case. Jim also happens to be one of the world's leading firefly researchers. Writing this book gave me a rare opportunity to write about the career of a remarkable scientist and a wonderful person. It also offered the chance to learn more about one of Earth's most dazzling creatures.

Jim Case is the author's stepfather and a scientist who studies fireflies.

"I began my research for this book by reading a variety of scientific articles that explained how fireflies make their light and how they use light to communicate with one another. Next, I flew to Santa Barbara, California, to visit my stepfather. He answered all my questions about his life and work.

"The most difficult part of writing this book was sticking to the topic of fireflies. Many fascinating ocean creatures make their own light too. I was often tempted to include information about them. But fireflies are so interesting that there was no room in this book to talk about other animals.

"If you've ever seen a firefly's tiny yellow-green flash, you will understand why may people think they are special. I hope the story you are about to read inspires you to enjoy the magic and mystery of fireflies the next time you see them on a hot, humid summer night."

Fireflies are just one of the many insects that live along rivers in Malaysia.

In Search of Fireflies

In the summer of 1979, Professor Jim Case waited alone on a platform in western Malaysia. The platform was perched among mangrove trees lining the edge of the Kuala Selangor River, about 6 miles (10 kilometers) from the Strait of Malacca.

Jim tried to keep still as he waited, but it wasn't easy. Thousands of biting ants swarmed over the platform and sank their jaws into his flesh. Mosquitoes also worried Jim. They carried a dreaded disease called Dengue fever, so Jim had to bundle up tight—not the most comfortable thing to do in the sweltering tropical heat.

To pass the time, Jim studied the wealth of wildlife around him. In the water, *venomous* snakes called kraits glided across the river's

Jim has often faced fighting ants and other harmful insects as he studies fireflies in the wild.

The great hornbill is one of the many spectacular birds Jim observed while working in Malaysia.

surface. Tropical birds dashed in and out of the mangrove trees and filled the air with their mysterious calls and songs. The wealth of insects astonished Jim. Besides the mosquitoes and ants, thousands of kinds of beetles, moths, dragonflies, and other insects crawled, fluttered, and chirped around him.

As the sun faded from the tropical sky, however, Jim's spirits rose. He checked his camera and flash to make sure everything was ready. Soon, one special insect would show itself—the insect Jim had traveled thousands of miles to study and learn more about. It was the firefly.

BRIGHT BEETLES

The light from fireflies—or "lightning bugs" as many people call them—has fascinated scientists for hundreds of years. In the 1850s, the famous naturalist Henry David Thoreau spent many hours trying to identify various fireflies in Massachusetts. Before and since, biologists all over the world have worked to learn as much as they can about these remarkable creatures.

Fireflies are not really flies. They are beetles. More than 2,000 kinds of fireflies roam our planet. About 170 kinds live in North America. Most are found along the East Coast. Florida and Georgia are especially firefly-rich. The warm, wet environments of these states provide especially good homes to the insects.

David Henry Thoreau was one of the first American naturalists to take an avid interest in fireflies.

FIREFLIES: THE FACTS	
KIND OF INSECT:	Beetle
SIZE:	½ to 1½ inches (1.3 to 3.8 centimeters)
FOOD:	Larvae eat worms, snails, and other small animals. Some adult fireflies eat other fireflies, but most feed on sugary plant juices.
LIFESPAN:	1 to 3 years as larvae, a few weeks or months as adults
FLIGHT SPEED:	1 to 3 miles (1.6 to 4.8 km) per hour

Like other beetles, fireflies have two life stages. Wormlike *larvae* hatch from eggs laid by female fireflies. The glowing larvae—often called "glowworms" —hunt tiny snails, worms, and other creatures. Eventually, they go through a series of changes called *metamorphosis* and become adult beetles.

Firefly larvae, or glowworms, have no wings, so they cannot fly.

The firefly's unique light organ sets it apart from other beetles.

The thing that sets a firefly apart from other kinds of beetles is its amazing light organ. This light organ is located under the tip of the firefly's tail. Not every kind of firefly comes equipped with a working light organ, but most do. Very few other land animals can make their own light. That is why many biologists, including Jim Case, find fireflies so interesting.

Jim Case (right) with his father

THE ROAD TO SCIENCE

JIM'S INTEREST IN HOW THINGS WORK STARTED early in life. He was born in 1926 in the small town of Bristow, Oklahoma, where his father ran the engineering plant for one of Oklahoma's first radio stations. Soon the family moved to Coffeyville, Kansas, for another radio-station job. Jim often visited the radio stations where his father worked. While his father operated and repaired the huge generating and transmitting machines, Jim spent his time figuring out how everything worked.

After several years in Coffeyville, the family moved to Bartlesville, Oklahoma. It was in Bartlesville that Jim's interest in nature and science began to gel.

"By the time I was in high school," Jim recalls, "I spent a lot of time collecting insects in the woods and fields around Bartlesville. In ninth or tenth grade, we had a biology teacher named Mr. Hamburger. We called him Happy Harry Hamburger.

"He had a totally insane way of teaching. He had a huge room full of biological specimens. During the

Jim's high school biology teacher, "Happy Harry Hamburger," made his students identify biological specimens over and over again.

year, we had to classify and label every one of them. Over the summer, Mr. Hamburger would take off all our labels so we had to start all over again the next year." Jim's experiences collecting and identifying animals taught him a lot about nature and inspired him to learn even more.

DROPPING IN, DROPPING OUT

Surprisingly, on his way to becoming a renowned scientist, Jim never graduated from high school— or from college. "I got into college by accident," he explains. "When I was still in high school, I got invited to a dance at the University of Kansas in Lawrence. The next morning, I saw a sign that said 'Entrance Examination.' I took the test and then went home. A few weeks later, I received a letter saying I could start college without graduating from high school."

Jim went to college at the University of Kansas. He was accepted even though he hadn't finished high school.

At the University of Kansas, Jim took a variety of courses that interested him, mostly in science. Unfortunately, after several years, Jim realized that he hadn't been taking enough required classes to graduate on time. Instead of finishing his undergraduate studies, Jim decided to apply to graduate school.

He was accepted by several leading universities, and he chose Johns Hopkins University in Baltimore, Maryland. Over the next 4 years, Jim earned his Ph.D., or doctorate degree, in *physiology* (fih-zee-AH-luh-jee)—the study of how the internal systems of animals and plants work. Afterward, he began a scientific career that would take him across the globe and allow him to study a huge variety of animals—including fireflies.

Around the time Jim was at Johns Hopkins University, this building served as the library.

HOW FIREFLIES USE THEIR LIGHTS

ON HIS WAY TO BECOMING A LEADING BIOLOGIST, Jim's life has taken many surprising twists. After graduating from Johns Hopkins, Jim was drafted into the United States Army to do research on insect physiology. In the army, he met John Buck—a man who would become his lifelong friend and research partner.

John Buck and Jim Case have known each other for many years. Here, John's wife, Elisabeth, helps him build a cage to hold fireflies.

"At the time," Jim explains, "I was trying to understand exactly how insects breathe. John had done a lot of work in this area, so I went over to see him. I didn't know he was interested in fireflies. Then, after I got out of the army, I was doing research at the Marine Biological Laboratory in

Woods Hole, Massachusetts. John was also there. One day, he was looking for someone to help him make a firefly light up. 'I'll help,' I said, and that started our work together."

Scientists already knew that fireflies make their light with a special chemical reaction. In this reaction, light is produced when a protein called *luciferin* (loo-SIH-fuh-ruhn) reacts with oxygen, a molecule called *ATP*, and an *enzyme* called *luciferase* (loo-SIH-fuh-rayz). Jim and John wanted to learn how a firefly turns on its light. To do this, they had to figure out which nerves carry messages from a firefly's brain to its light organ.

Jim and John first studied fireflies at the Marine Biological Laboratory in Woods Hole, Massachusetts.

How does a firefly's nervous system work? Jim and John spent several years unraveling its secrets.

The two scientists spent several years measuring the electrical patterns that travel through a firefly's nerves when the insect sees light and when it flashes. Using this information, Jim and John created an overall picture of how a firefly's nervous system works. As he worked, Jim also became interested in how a firefly uses its light.

DATING WITH LIGHTS

Many ocean animals make their own light. They use it to hide from enemies, catch *prey*, and find one another. Most fireflies use their lights to attract mates.

To find a mate, a male firefly begins flying at dusk. He flashes his light every few seconds. When he spots a female's flash, he begins flying toward her. Females usually perch on plants or on the ground. If the female is ready to mate, she keeps flashing every time she sees a flash from the male. Eventually, the male lands next to her, and they mate.

Fireflies use their light to communicate with each other during mating.

Each kind of firefly has its own "flash code" for mating. Some males may flash twice and the female responds by flashing once. Other males glow continuously while the female gives out a series of single flashes.

The length of a flash, the time between flashes, and the color of the light are also important to fireflies. Together with the flash code, these features allow dozens of different kinds of fireflies to tell each other apart and attract only their own kind.

TALKING TO FIREFLIES

If fireflies are common where you live, you can try "talking" to them. Go out at dusk with a penlight. When you see a flying male flash, flash back to him. To learn the proper flash code, look for females sitting on the ground or on branches. Use the same codes they flash. You could also try this common flash code: Whenever a flying male flashes, wait 2 seconds, then flash back at him for 1 second. If you "talk right," he'll think you're his mate and start flying toward you.

Different kinds of fireflies use different flash codes to communicate.

During the 1960s, Jim spent his summers working to understand how fireflies communicate with their flash codes. He also looked at how male and female fireflies see each other's light. Soon, though, Jim encountered something that took his research in a dazzling new direction.

Jim Case standing outside of a hut used as a field laboratory during his trip to Papua New Guinea.

The Fireflies of Southeast Asia

IN 1969, JIM TOOK AN EXCITING JOURNEY ABOARD a research ship called the *Alpha Helix*. During the trip, he and more than a dozen other scientists traveled throughout Southeast Asia. While visiting the highlands of Papua New Guinea, Jim encountered something he'd never seen before—large groups of fireflies that all flash at the same time. These fireflies—called *synchronous* (SIN-kroh-nuhs) fireflies—amazed Jim. Soon they began to play a major role in his firefly research.

More than 300 years ago, European explorers brought back reports of Southeast Asia's magical synchronous fireflies. It wasn't until the mid-1960s, however, that John Buck and other biologists began seriously studying these insects.

At least half a dozen kinds of Asian fireflies are synchronous. Every night, large numbers of these fireflies gather in trees or bushes, usually along rivers. As dusk closes in, the fireflies begin flashing at random. But soon, the male fireflies all begin flashing at the same time.

Asia's synchronous fireflies gather along the rivers at dusk.

Some kinds of synchronous fireflies flash every 2 or 3 seconds. Others flash every half second. The results are spectacular. Along rivers in Thailand and Malaysia, hundreds of thousands of fireflies flash together, creating awesome light shows. In some places, the fireflies flash until midnight or later, attracting firefly-watchers from all over the world.

For Jim Case, John Buck, and other scientists, these light shows raise an important question: Why?

FANTASTIC FLASHING

Most scientists believe that synchronous fireflies—like other fireflies—flash to find mates. However, flashing together may give synchronous fireflies a special advantage in the thick forests where they live. In an article in *Scientific American* magazine, John Buck explains that for fireflies to mate, a male and female must be able to see each other's flashes the entire time the male is flying toward the female. If a tree or some other object gets between the male and female, the two fireflies often stop signaling to each other and do not mate.

Flashing together in large numbers may make it much easier for fireflies to find each other in thick jungle areas. If many males flash at the same time, John reasons, they create a beacon of light that is bright enough to attract females and other males over great distances and from all directions. This may help males find more females than if they were just patrolling the forest on their own.

John's *theory* seems to make sense. When scientists first started thinking about synchronous fireflies, however, they had one big problem—no one had ever seen two synchronous fireflies mate! Jim Case decided to try to solve this problem by studying one kind of synchronous firefly that lives in Malaysia.

FIREFLY SAFARI

In the summer of 1979, Jim flew to the city of Kuala Lumpur and made his way to the Kuala Selangor River. He joined a group of Malaysian researchers

A Malaysian guide transports Jim and a graduate student down the Kuala Selangor River.

Jim spent many hours on this platform observing and photographing synchronous fireflies.

who had built an observation platform along the river. For the next few weeks, Jim spent his time observing and photographing synchronous fireflies.

Studying the insects turned out to be more difficult than Jim had expected. It seemed that whenever he tried to photograph a male firefly, the wind would blow the branch the insect was resting on. Jim also had trouble keeping track of individual fireflies because they often flashed in groups.

The biting insects and stifling heat made Jim's work extremely uncomfortable too. "To top it off," Jim adds, "my camera equipment was pretty poor for doing low light-level photography at close range. I didn't have good camera lenses for it."

SECRET SYNCHRONOUS LIVES

After 10 long days on the river, Jim finally took some good photos of what he was looking for—mating fireflies. When females see all the males flashing at the same time, each one flashes back individually. Females do not flash synchronously. This allows a male to pinpoint the location of one particular female and fly to her.

To court the female, the male crawls up behind her and climbs up onto her back. He taps the female's back end with his legs and, at the same time, twists his light organ around so that it flashes directly over the female's eyes.

The male often waves his light back and forth in front of her eyes and sways his body from side to side. "While the male is doing this," Jim observes, "the female may stand quietly, or she may walk around. She may light up, or she may not."

Soon, the male tries to mate with the female. If she allows it, they mate tail-to-tail and stay in that position for several hours.

What Jim saw was unlike anything anyone had ever observed before. "Really," he recalls, "it was so bizarre that I was just beside myself to photograph it. I knew that nobody would believe me if I just described it."

During courtship, a male synchronous firefly sometimes climbs on top of his mate and shines his light organ in her eyes.

To further convince other scientists of what he saw, Jim brought some synchronous fireflies back to his laboratory in the United States. To his delight, the fireflies courted and mated in the laboratory just as they had in Malaysia.

PUTTING TOGETHER THE PIECES OF A PUZZLE

Jim's discoveries don't completely explain why synchronous fireflies flash together, but they provide important clues to the answer. As John Buck suggests, flashing together probably helps an entire population of synchronous fireflies find one another. But Jim's work shows that other factors may be more important in how an individual male finds and "wins" a female.

By shining his light into the female's eyes, for instance, the male prevents the female from seeing other males. This probably increases the chances that she will mate with this male. It's one more piece of the fascinating firefly puzzle that Jim and other scientists are working to put together.

Jim's discoveries in the field and at the University of California, Santa Barbara have added a great deal to what scientists know about firefly mating.

Many ocean creatures, such as this
sea jelly, make their own light.

THE RESEARCH CONTINUES

AS MUCH AS JIM ENJOYS WORKING WITH FIREFLIES, they aren't the only animals he has studied. He has also done research on ocean creatures that make their own light and spent time studying the ability of animals to detect odors, tastes, and other chemicals in air and water. No matter what Jim works on, he has the same philosophy about his research. "I don't have a huge plan for my life," he explains. "I see something, and I just get this feeling that it's something interesting that I should look at."

Jim retired from the University of California at Santa Barbara in 1997. By that time, he had been a professor for more than 35 years and a vice-chancellor of research for almost 10 years. He had also trained dozens of future scientists. Although Jim retired from his job, he didn't stop being a scientist —not by a long shot. Now he is busier than ever. He spends his time working on whatever interests him.

As a child, Jim enjoyed tinkering with the equipment at the radio stations where his father worked.

For Jim, research is fun. Here, he listens to a firefly and tries to count how fast its wings are beating.

Today, many years later, he still enjoys building equipment and trying to figure out how things work. "A lot of my work involves building equipment that might help scientists to learn something new about a particular animal or a particular biological process," says Jim.

THE WIND TUNNEL

One piece of equipment that Jim recently built is a kind of mini-wind tunnel for insects. When Jim places a firefly in the machine, the insect thinks it is flying. How does Jim trick the insect? He begins by gluing a small piece of balsa wood to the firefly's back. Then he attaches the firefly to a small, rotating device and uses a fan to blow "wind" over the animal. Jim knows his setup is successful because the firefly begins flapping its wings and changing directions as though it is flying.

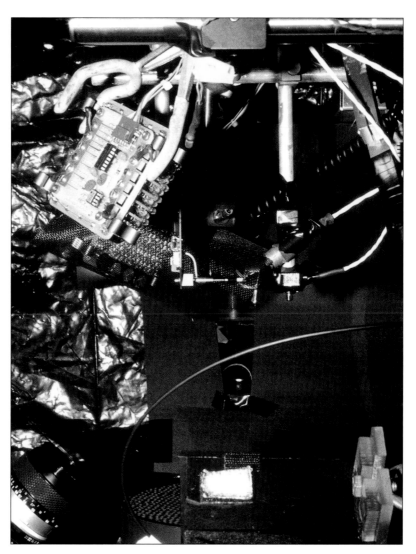

Jim built this wind tunnel himself. He uses it to study fireflies in flight.

This firefly thinks it is flying through the air. It doesn't know it is anchored to Jim's device.

The wind tunnel allows Jim to study how fireflies behave in flight. Since most fireflies are active only in dim light, it is impossible to get the same kind of information outside the lab. The wind-tunnel setup includes a number of small lights that flash on and off—just like fireflies. By using a computer, Jim can control how often and how long each light flashes. Then he can watch how the fireflies respond.

"One thing we've learned," Jim says, "is how persistent the males can be in pursuing a female. For example, if you get a male flying in a particular direction toward a flashing female, and you suddenly turn off the female's light, some males will keep flying for 10 to 15 minutes before they realize they aren't going to reach the female.

"We also tried to get a male firefly to change course from one female to another. If a male was flying toward one flashing 'female,' we flashed a light from a different direction. It turns out that if the second light is bright enough, the male will quit flying toward the first 'female' and fly toward the second light instead."

FIREFLIES AT RISK

As wonderful as fireflies are, many firefly populations are in danger. They need moist areas to live and reproduce. Whenever a wetland is destroyed, many fireflies may lose their home. Artificial lights that draw male fireflies away from females can also cause problems.

In Asia, synchronous fireflies are threatened by new dam projects that will flood the rivers where the insects breed. The government of Malaysia is trying to find a solution to this problem because the fireflies have become an important tourist attraction.

THE VALUE OF RESEARCH

Jim knows that his work may not change the world, but he believes that all research is valuable. "As humans, it's our obligation to ask questions and find answers," he says. "Some people think and find if something doesn't directly affect them, they don't need to know about it." That attitude bothers me.

"Pure science is like investing for the future," Jim continues. "We never know when pure science is going to turn out to be extremely valuable. That's been proven over and over. It's important to understand nature even if we can't predict how that knowledge is going to help us."

As research on human genes has shown, pure science often helps us in ways we cannot predict.

Passion and an interest in the world—these are the two main things a young person needs to become a scientist.

That's why Jim believes that young people who are interested in science should follow their dreams. More than anything, he says, it is passion that drives the best scientists he knows. Whether they study the human body, deep-sea animals, or fluttering fireflies, the best biologists are those who *want* to learn more about the world around them. Do you have that desire to learn? If the answer is 'yes,' you're well on your way to becoming a biologist too.

IMPORTANT WORDS

ATP   (noun) a molecule that stores and releases the energy that drives many of the body processes that make it possible for a creature to live and grow

enzyme   (noun) a kind of protein that can speed up a chemical reaction

larva   (noun) the first stage in the life of some animals. The plural is *larvae*.

luciferase   (noun) an enzyme that allows fireflies and many ocean creatures to make light

luciferin   (noun) a protein that produces light when it is broken down during a chemical reaction

metamorphosis   (noun) a series of changes that some young animals go through as they become adults

physiology   (noun) the branch of biology that studies how the bodies of plants and animals work *prey* (noun) an animal that is hunted and killed for food by another animal

synchronous (adjective) happening at the same time

theory (noun) an idea that is supported by some evidence, but has not been proven

venomous (adjective) able to inject a poisonous fluid into prey and enemies

TO FIND OUT MORE

BOOKS

Ganeri, Anita. *Creatures that Glow*. New York: Harry N. Abrams, Inc., 1995.

Gerber, Carole. *Firefly Night*. New York: Whispering Coyote Press, 2000.

Munan, Heidi. *Malaysia*. Tarrytown, NY: Benchmark Books, 1994.

Pascoe, Elaine. *Beetles*. Woodbridge, CT: Blackbirch Press, 2000.

Presnall, Judith Janda. *Animals That Glow*. New York: Franklin Watts, 1993.

MAGAZINE ARTICLES

Schneider, Dan. "How Do Fireflies Do It?" *Canadian Geographic*. June/July 1990.

Tweit, Susan J. "Dance of the Fireflies," *Audubon*. July/August 1999.

Lambeth, Ellen. "Lights Alive," *Ranger Rick*. January 1999.

The Fireflyer Companion

http://gnv.ifas.ufl.edu/~jlloyd/ffdoc.html

At this site, you can read back issues of a newsletter devoted to firefly news, history, and research.

The Firefly Files

http://IRIS.biosci.ohio-state.edu:80/projects/FFiles/

Sponsored by the Museum of Biological Diversity at Ohio State University, this site offers basic information, references, and activities relating to fireflies.

James F. Case

http://lifesci.ucsb.edu/~case

This Web page describes the research and career of Professor James Case. It is part of the University of California at Santa Barbara's Web site.

State Insect for Indiana

http://www.entm.purdue.edu/Entomology/outreach/firefly/index.htm

A growing number of people in Indiana are interested in adopting the firefly as their state insect. This site has all kinds of interesting information about fireflies.

Wildlife Conservation Society

http://www.wcs.org

2300 Southern Blvd.
Bronx, NY 10460-1099

INDEX

PHOTOGRAPHS©: Animals Animals/H. Taylor/OSF: 10; AP/Wide World Photos: 17, 18, 20, 21; Corbis-Bettmann: 11; Courtesy of James Case: 14, 30, 31, 38, 39, 40; Minden Pictures/Mark Moffett: 9 bottom; Peter Arnold Inc.: 25 (Keith Kent), 12 (S.J. Krasemann), 36 (Sea Studios, Inc.); Photo Researchers, NY: 23 (Scott Camazine), 16 (Scott Camazine/Sue Trainor), cover (E.R. Degginger), cover background, 1, border art, 6 (Fletcher & Baylis), 42 (James King-Holmes/SPL), 32 (Doug Martin); Photodisc, Inc.: 9 top, 15, 19 top, 37, 46; Robert & Linda Mitchell: 8, 28; Sneed B. Collard III: 19 bottom (John B. Buck), 7, 26, 33, 35; Visuals Unlimited: backcover, 13, 22, 27, 44, 45 (Jeff J. Daly), 43 (Jeff Greenberg).

92
CAS

Collard, Sneed B.

A firefly biologist
at work.

WITHDRAWN

35793000278498

$22.50